Answers About The Afterlife

A Companion to *The Love Never Ends*

Sunny Dawn Johnston

:

This book is dedicated to those curious enough to ask questions about the Afterlife, those open enough to hear the answers and anyone on the journey of discovering your connections with the Spirit World.

Contents

Introduction

The topic of the afterlife is one of absolute extremes that most people have an opinion about.

As a Psychic Medium with over 30 years of experience, I am answering these questions based on my own personal experience with the Afterlife. Years of questions that my clients, friends, and students have asked me, and their loved ones in Spirit, throughout the years. These answers are in no particular order and were usually asked in response to this question:

If you could have one question answered about death or what happens during or after you die, what would it be?

The following answers are from my own personal experience and observation. They are based on communication, interpretation and conversation I've had over the years with the Spirit world. My intention in sharing them with you is not to say this is the right way, but to simply answer common questions based on MY experience.

The questions are grouped by topic. Some answers are more detailed than others. For many of these topics, it is most helpful to read all responses in a particular section to get an overall feel for my answer.

~ Blessings to you on your journey with the Afterlife

~ Sunny Dawn Johnston

Answers About the Afterlife

What does the transition "feel" like? I get a lot of different responses to this question from the Other Side. The most common is that it feels the same as it does when you go to sleep.

Do you feel pain during transition? You feel no pain at the point of transition. It is a complete and absolute release of resistance. That doesn't mean that people don't feel pain during the death process, but at the point of transition, no.

Is there truly an overwhelming feeling of peace?? Yes. Spirits usually report back that they felt an intense sense of peace and love. They experience feelings that can't even be described in words... they usually show me color... color that I haven't seen before with my physical eyes.

In deaths that are premature (accident, murder, etc. of someone still young) is there a moment of conscious choice to let go vs. fight to stay? I don't know if I would say a conscious choice, but I would say that there is a moment where the Spirit recognizes that it is either time to turn back or to continue forward on the journey home.

The thing that scares me about the dying process is NOT BREATHING! Are people suffocating? The last breaths are so labored and appear horrible. Is the person in pain? Panic? Where are they when the breathing becomes so hard? Yes, sometimes they are suffocating. The reality is that the way we leave this physical existence can be traumatizing and painful to the physical shell. The feedback I get from the Spirit world is that during these times, they go in and out of the body. So, when you are with someone and they seem to not be there, it's because oftentimes they aren't. When the breathing becomes so labored it is often referred to as the death rattle. The death rattle can be very difficult for both the person passing as well as the loved ones watching. During the death rattle, one suggestion that might help to calm everyone down is to hold that person's hand, and get into sync with their breath - becoming one breath. I was taught this technique in hospice training with Dannion Brinkley and it has been a fabulous tool.

Can you tell when someone is going to pass, even if they aren't sick?? There are some mediums that tune into that more than others. I have had experiences where I have felt that, for some unknown reason, but it is not common for me.

At what point does the soul actually leave the body during the dying phase? Just before the heart stops and the body dies, or moments or a time before? The Spirit can come and go, throughout our lives - visit the Other Side, check out when we are in pain… but when the heart quits beating, the Spirit has gone home.

When I die, is there heartache? Will I feel sadness or loss for those I am not able to physically be with on Earth? It depends. If you desire to stay more connected to your loved ones then you can tune into their frequency, and feel their sadness. This is often the case when you first transition and are still in what I refer to as a healing space. Once you have transcended that area, then it is likely that you would not feel their sadness or pain, but rather just feel love, regardless of what you are observing in them.

What happens at the moment of death? At the moment of death, we release all resistance and form.

What is on the other side of this life? Where do we go? Eternity!!! I get different answers from different Spirits; therefore I have come to believe that we go to where we believe we will go and we create whatever it is we want to create. The stories vary greatly.

Who will be there to help me cross over? Those that you have loved that have already crossed over will be there, waiting for you. This can be family members, friends, colleagues, and even your beloved animals. Anyone that you loved, can be there. In addition, you will become aware of your Guardian Angel and your Spirit Guides if you weren't already.

When one transitions alone, do they hear and know you got there too late? Do they still feel your love? They absolutely feel your love… and your guilt. It is best if you can try to focus on your love. If you got there too late, then that was part of the Divine plan, which they now know. So, yes, they know you tried to get there; and oftentimes, honestly, they don't want anyone there. They want to be alone. The way it is often revealed to me, and as I share in Jimmy's story in my book, is that it will be the way they want it. So if you are there, or not, it is in perfect Divine order.

Can you 'feel' a loved one's Spirit move through you at the time of death, even if you are not physically with them? Yes, when someone dies it is possible to feel their Spirit move through you at their time of death, even if you are not with them. When you have a strong love connection, and the physical presence leaves, many people feel them leave. Some are even awakened out of a deep sleep or see their Spirits as they leave.

What happens during the burial process? The Spirit leaves the body at the time of death. They are not attached to the body at that point. Therefore, the burial process is a sacred experience for those of us living. The deceased loved one will be at the burial, but they have no connection to the body at that point. It is a shell, being put into the earth, not unlike a snake that sheds it's skin. It is of no purpose to them any longer.

Do our loved ones attend their own funeral? Absolutely, your loved ones are with you throughout the process- whether it is a burial, a cremation, a ceremony or a celebration. They will be there, offering that Love that connected you with them originally.

What does it mean when you are viewing the body of a deceased person and you see white

energy coming out of it? I personally haven't experienced this, but when I see white around the living, it means that they are at peace. I don't believe it would mean anything different.

What is this horrible fear I get about death... like a "there is nothing after I die" feeling? Especially at night when just falling asleep! My thought is that it is the ingrained fear of the unknown that takes you over. It's interesting, because the Spirit world has told me that dying is much like going to sleep. Some Spiritual teachers even suggested that we die every night, when we "leave" our bodies for the dream state. So, my thought is that you have a deep seated fear within you, that you will die, and never wake up to anything. It is my hope and intention that my book will help you to release some of this fear.

Should I fear death and the afterlife? No, this life is much scarier than the afterlife. Death can be as simple as just taking a breath. I think what causes some of the fear is the unknown. We as humans have fear in the things we don't see or know or understand.

Know that you are eternal, and death is as natural as birth. When someone dies here, it is birth and celebration there. And when someone dies there, it is birth and celebration here.

I would like to know why some people fear death, myself being one of them. I know we plan our life out so I know that our soul must not fear it, but why as a human vessel is that a fear for us? I believe the fear is there because when we are born, we get some sort of amnesia of all that our soul knows. We spend this life remembering those things that we know on an intuitive soul level. So, we can be afraid because we have forgotten why we are here. And oftentimes when we begin to remember, we tell ourselves "Oh, that is too easy. It must be harder than that." I also believe that we are also trained to be fearful, by our society at large... and not trained to trust; therefore, the fear feels more natural and can be stronger.

Why are some animals/people afraid of dying when they are going through the transition process and some are not? One BIG reason is because we have been taught that it is the end. That death is the end of life. It is not. It is a change - a change into a new form.

How do I help someone transition without fear?
Share with them what you have learned from my
book. Help them to understand that love never ends
and that they will still be with you, just from another
point of view. Teach them about the absolutely
blissful place they are going to: the beautiful light
vibration that words cannot even express, the sounds
that are so powerful that you just can't get enough
and the love...that is out of this world. Once you
have shared, you must then let them find their own
way, and honor that way. Whether they go in fear or
they go in love, love is on the other side. That could
bring you both some peace.

**I've been with different family members when
they are very near their time of crossing over and
they all spend time looking upward at something.
Are they seeing Angels or the light of angels or
what? They don't talk about it, as I've asked
them what are they looking at and they don't
answer.** Yes, they are seeing light beings. It could be
Angels, Deceased Loved Ones, Spirit Guides, or a
Guardian Angel. Everyone has a different experience

so there isn't a one-size-fits-all answer. The best answer I would say is that they are all connecting to the Spirit world, recognizing it in some form. Sometimes they do speak about it, or reach out to touch it.

It seems so unfair...Why must some people that have truly lived as a human angel suffer a long and painful death? Things seem unfair in this human realm because we don't see the bigger picture. It is hard to understand with our limited human perception, as we base things on good and bad, right and wrong. From all of my experiences with the Spirit world, this one thing is true. They left in the perfect way for them and their legacy. Meaning, that whether it was good or bad, in our perception, it was purposeful for their journey... and likely for the journey of those that loved them as well.

How does a Soul release from this earthly plane? The best way that I can describe what I have felt and seen is it is almost like it is sucked up, like a vacuum. Remember that the Spirit is energy (nonphysical), so there is no form. It's as if that energy shoots up this light vibrational suction cup or tube of sorts. The tube is complete light... awe inspiring, indescribable, vibrating beams of brilliant light. The light feels to me like absolute love and healing.

I was a Hospice Social Worker for 6 years and helped over 500 people transition. For most of my patients and no matter how much they were suffering during the dying process, there was a "peace" that came over their faces moments before their hearts actually stopped. Some would even open their eyes with that peace. What happens at that point? Are they experiencing something in the physical that makes it easier for them to let go? Are they experiencing something so their loved one watching can let go? I don't know if I would say they are experiencing something in the physical that makes it easier to let go; or whether moments before they leave, they see and feel the energy of the Spirit world as described in the above question that allows them to release their resistance at that point. It's almost as though it is the body acknowledging their freedom. Yes, this "peace" is often the expression that is left for the family members to witness and hopefully carry with them.

During my hospice volunteer work I saw several people that were in comas near the end of their life and it seemed as if their Spirit was going in and out of the body. A few of them had some unresolved family issues. Do most people hang on for as long as they can in the hope of resolving things before they pass? It can be that they are waiting to give family members or friends the opportunity to resolve issues beforehand, yes. It can also be that they are doing some of their own work before they transition. The truth is, there are times where we will not understand why they are hanging on for so long, as in the case of Jimmie's story in my book. It can be very difficult to witness, especially if they are perceived to be in pain. WE have to find a way to trust that all is in Divine time. If we are divine beings, God Sparks, Spirit embodied, then we know, on a soul level, when it is time to go. We as humans have to learn to believe that as well.

I lost my amazing Dad at 12:02am and 3 days later at 12:05am my beautiful Mum suffered a massive stroke and died as well. Bearing in mind she had Alzheimer's and didn't even know Dad was ill, do you believe my Dad went to get my Mum? The disease of the body is lifted once we pass over, so Alzheimer's does not affect her Spirit as it transcends this physical earth. Yes, I would believe that your father would be there to receive your mom, even though he had only passed over a few days earlier. Remember, the Spirit is no longer in a body. The Spirit world is mental, so as soon as he thinks about being with her he can be, and he can be in more than one place at once as well.

When my grandma passed, it was a two day process and during that time she talked about seeing an Angel at the foot of her bed, my grandpa who had gone ten years before her, as well as her siblings that had been gone a long time....are those who went before really there waiting for us? We talk about "I will see you again when my time comes" but is this really true that we do see them again? Yes, it is absolutely true that we see them again. They are there to greet us once we transition and celebrate our birthday (the day of death in this physical world is a day of birth in Spirit world) … our coming back home.

Is there something called in limbo or like a purgatory? Or maybe they have to serve penance for something they did wrong in this life time? It has never been my experience that there is any type of purgatory or place of penance, even for what we would call the worst people. My experience is one of light and love, growth, awareness and expansion. Those that we might assume go to purgatory, receive the same healing energies, love and support in the Spirit world as those that are worshipped as enlightened beings or wise men in the physical world.

I think I understand a little bit about becoming a Spirit after transitioning, so how long before you become a Spirit? Does everyone become a Spirit? You already are a Spirit, it is simply embodied. Meaning, your Spirit enters your body when you are born and when your body dies, your Spirit leaves your body to go back home. Yes, everyone is a Spirit and follows this same journey.

What are ghosts? Are they something to fear? Ghosts are just Spirits that pass away and are not ready to go to the light yet. They can be unaware that they have passed away or they still feel the need to stay close, for a variety of reasons. Usually it is because they feel they have some kind of unfinished business of sorts.

Do we die alone?? You do not die alone, even if you are seemingly alone in this physical world. You have your Guardian Angels and Spirit Guides right beside you, just like you did during your birth here. They are beside you throughout your entire journey. Once you transition, your loved ones, animals, friends and other light beings are also there with you. So no, you do not die alone.

Is there really an afterlife? Yes, life and love are infinite. The afterlife is your creation. You are a vibrational, energetic being constantly creating and expanding. Yes, the afterlife is real.

Do you truly have a consciousness after you pass? I'm not afraid of dying; I'm afraid of the end truly being just that... The End. That is a fear that many people have. I have had encounters with thousands of deceased energies and would say that there is no evidence that there is an END!

Where is the Other Side? It is here and there and everywhere. I have never been able to get an address, per se. It is everywhere. It's in the stars and walking along side us. It's literally everywhere.

What happens to the BAD people? They go to the same place as everyone else. We can call it heaven if you like, they just go to a lower vibrational space.

Does the version of afterlife we get depend on what we believe? The Spirit world is a mental world. It is based on thought. So, yes, the thoughts you think will create your afterlife experiences. In addition, once there, you learn and grow. Your initial thoughts begin to expand as well, creating new experiences beyond what you believed in the physical world.

Do you meet God? Yes. You are an aspect of God, a thumbprint of the Divine, and so in essence you and God are one and the same. It takes the human mind a bit of time to wrap their heads around this one sometimes. It has been my experience over and over again that we ARE the Divine, the Creator. Like a drop of water in the ocean: Is it a drop of water, or is it the ocean? Each individual drop creates the ocean, just as each individual soul creates the Divine. So, in truth, you have already met, because you are one in the same.

What is heaven? Does it really exist? I believe that Heaven is where we go when we leave our bodies. There are varying degrees of heaven, based on vibration. Therefore, we go to the level that we vibrate to based on our thoughts, words and actions when we were in physical form. Those that were of a high vibration in the physical realm will be in a higher vibration in the Spirit realm. Those that were in a lower vibration in the physical world will be in a lower vibration in the Spirit world as well. So, we will be with beings that are of the same vibrational resonance as we are. Simply said, we will hang with the energies of those that are on the same level of spiritual evolution as we are.

What does heaven looks like? Heaven looks like whatever you want it to look like. It is based on your thoughts. I see it as similar to our physical earth, but with much brighter light and intense colors and sounds; colors and sounds that cannot be explained with human words.

What about our senses? Gone?... The smell of good food cooking, flowers & babies?... What

about belly laughs with friends?... Getting physical: Jumping for joy? Having fun? Romance? Good food and good company with friends and loved ones? Good books? Good shows? Great songs? Life and time on the planet? Sure would miss it! I am told that all of these and more exist in the Spirit world, just not in the same form that we have them here ... and that although we feel like we would miss it because it is what we know right now, going home is so much better than we could ever imagine with our human mind. And, once there, we would not consider coming back... except for the carrot of future expansion and contrast dangling in front of us.

Can humans become Guardian Angels, especially for children? Well, not technically Angels. Humans that have transitioned can become a Guardian or a Spirit Guide for them. They don't become Angels. Angels are a high vibrational being that doesn't incarnate into a physical body; and a physical body doesn't become an Angel. However, all humans already have Guardian Angels that guide and support them throughout their evolution.

Will I remember my life? Yes, you will remember your life, especially immediately. I am told though, that everyone has different experiences and so there is not a one-size-fits-all answer. As you expand and grow, your memory becomes more distant. I can't say that it isn't remembered, but more that it isn't focused upon. It's kind of like when you practice for a test, and you remember everything, and then the further away you get from the test, the less attention there is on it. Not because it isn't important, but because you are now focused on something new. You can remember it, when something triggers it, but it isn't necessarily in your awareness any longer. Remember, we are trying to use human words and explanations for something that is not human, so the words won't always fit what they are trying to say to us.

Did I make the right decisions? You spend a lot of time once you have passed reviewing what you did on earth so you can learn and grow and expand. I believe in this space, it isn't about right and wrong. It is about how you have expanded.

Is there a life review after we have passed on? Yes, there is a life review. It is like as they go through their life review, they are witnessing everything that ever happened in their life... every feeling, every emotion, every experience. It is as if it is played out on a movie screen. I've been told that it's like you have a remote and you can fast forward and rewind through different parts of it afterwards. You can also see the way things might have turned out had you gone down a different road, or made a different choice. It is my understanding that one road isn't better than another. They generally all wind up going to the same place. It is really just more about the experience and the expansion of the person. As you go through this life review, there is no judge and jury. There is no one to condemn you. It is an opportunity to study the life you lived, and learn and grow from it with a new and different perspective. Because you are now in Spirit, you can see from a higher vibration and can see what each experience was truly about.

How do you fix any wrongs that you or another party think you did? I believe it depends on where you go. If you are in a healing space, then you work on forgiveness and releasing the pain and sadness that you carry. You also heal from the pain you caused others while in this state. If however, you are in a different state when you die, then it may not be necessary to go to a healing space (I don't know how this is decided.) At that point, the awareness of how nothing was ever actually wrong infuses you, and all is well.

When we die, do we receive all the answers to the questions we asked while living? At some point along the journey, yes, but not always immediately.

Will I see my loved ones again?!? Absolutely, you will. Anyone that you had a heart connection with you will have the choice to connect with again.

Would I know my family in heaven? Yes, you would recognize them vibrationally, as everything is vibration first.

Will I get to see or feel my parents...my children? Yes, if you choose to.

Will I see the ones who have passed before me? Will they be the age they were when they died? My dad was 51, I was 25. Now I'm 52, will he know me? Yes, you will see them but I use the word see, and it is more like a feeling or knowing. The Spirit world is a mental world. It is all thought based, so it is a recognition of them, based on their energy more than it is a vision of them based on their looks or age.

Will I miss my friends and family that I left behind? From what I hear, no. Not because you don't care, but because, when you transition, you are still with them if you desire to be. So, how or why would you miss friends and family, when they are right there with you?

If my deceased husband was married and widowed before marrying me, what will happen when I die… is he with his first wife in heaven? It is important to remember, we are no longer in a body when we return to the Spirit world. So there is no physical limitation. And, LOVE never ends. So, you can be with either or both, based on your desire. Looking at it from a human perspective, it seems as though we have to choose, one or the other; but we do not have those limitations in the Spirit world. So, literally you could be with both. There is no jealousy either, just LOVE.

Will I be a part of the lives of those still living?
That is up to the individual Spirit, but generally, yes.
If there are things that are of interest to you
happening in their lives, then you certainly would stay
connected to them. Sometimes, as time goes on and
people move through the healing process, it isn't as
necessary. But if you want to, yes, you can.

**Are you still able to visit and look after the ones
you leave behind?** Yes, you absolutely can visit and
look after your loved ones after you pass away. It is as
easy as a thought.

Can Spirit feel emotions of their loved ones? The
Spirit world connects with us through thoughts and
feelings; so yes, they can tune into our emotions.

**Do you have instant knowledge/memories of all
the lives you've lived once you cross over?** Once
you return to Spirit, you have knowledge of all that
you are and all that you have been. You may not
choose to focus on it; but yes, you are aware of all
aspects of your soul or all expressions of your Divine
light.

What are your relationships like once you pass? If you were married to someone or in a long-term loving relationship prior to death does it continue after both of you die? I wouldn't say a marriage continues, as marriage is a human experience. But, does the heart connection... the love, continue on? Yes it does. Over and over, many times with many different beings throughout lifetimes.

Do some people want to go back to their earthly life after death, especially when they feel they have unfinished business? Absolutely, there are souls that want to return to earth to "fix" things or to help people to heal, etc. And, they do come back, in Spirit form, to share those messages. It is up to us to listen so that they don't have to stay here longer than necessary, and so that they can move on in their new experience.

Does a person's grudge against another die with that person, or does the Spirit hold on to this energy? Typically, once someone passes, they "understand" the life experiences; therefore, any grudge would be gone. However, if they are in a low vibrational place, they may hold onto it for a time. As their healing occurs and they evolve a bit more, then the energy of the "grudge" would be healed as well. I have had a few experiences with the later, as they have shared with me from the other side.

When I pass will I be able to see family and will the same things that hurt me to see while I was here still hurt to see when I am gone? (For example, as in the way my favorite things were treated by others...) My experience has been that the majority of the time, the Spirits no longer care about the material things. They are in a much stronger vibration of love, so the things that once mattered, no longer do. This is not all of the time, but most of the time.

How can I communicate with my loved ones? The most important factor is to be **present**, so that you can see and feel, hear and know the messages that are happening all around you.

How soon are we able to communicate back with loved ones? The answer is immediately. There are a lot of "stories" out there that say you have to wait a certain amount of time, but that is not the case. You can communicate with them immediately if you are able to raise your vibration and be open. Or you could go to a medium like me. Bottom line, Spirit is always Spirit. We just receive a body when we are here and leave it when we go… we communicate all the while. No "on hold" time.

What is the one thing we can do to 'hear' them more clearly? Raise your vibration. That is the fastest way to communicate with them. Also, a lot of times it is helpful to be able to do some psychometry (the ability to obtain information about a person or event by touching an object related to that person or event) with an item of theirs. That can help connect you with their energy. Mostly, get into a place of feeling your love for them... and you will "hear" them.

Am I weird because I don't want to communicate with my dead loved ones? No, many people are uninterested in communicating with their loved ones for a variety of reason. It is ok if you don't... they won't take it personally.

When communicating with the Other Side: when a person calls out another person's name before they die - are they actually seeing that "dead"

person? Yes, typically they are there to welcome them to the Other Side. Remember that death here, is birth there; and they are awaiting the birth.

When someone crosses over, why does it take them a few months to get in contact with us? It doesn't. They can communicate with us immediately. It takes a lining up of energy, and that can take some time. It doesn't have to take time, but it can.

I've had two very close family members (brother and father) pass away. I can feel someone around, but how do I figure out WHO is trying to communicate with me? This can be challenging. It takes discernment, which is not something that can be taught. It must be experienced. So, it takes practice. First, I would ask and see if you get a clear sense of who it is. Sometimes it is that easy. Second, when you feel the presence of Spirit, tune into who comes into your heart and mind first, because that is likely correct. Your first hit with your intuition is usually right on. Third, ask for confirmation. Ask Spirit to show you a sign that it is the person you are thinking of...and then pay attention. This confirmation can be something like having their picture fall off the wall, or someone will call you with the same name, or you'll be driving and see a license plate that reminds you of them. If you ask for a sign, and pay attention to your intuition, Spirit will provide you with the validation.

Why do some people communicate with their loved ones when they pass and others don't? How do the ones who pass choose whom they relay messages through? This is a great question that I don't really understand myself. Sometimes, I think that they are focused elsewhere. Sometimes, it is because they feel like their communication will not serve a higher purpose or is unnecessary at that given time. Now, who they come through, that is different. Remember that it is easier for them to connect with those of a higher vibration, so they will come to people that can see and feel and hear and know them more easily... so that they don't have to lower their vibration any more in order to communicate with a physical person. So, they go to the people with the least resistance and the higher vibration. This is often why they come during the dream state - our vibration is high and we lack resistance at that time.

Why do you get often and consistent messages/communication from one person and not another? There are a variety of reasons why you might have communication with one and not another. Each Spirit has its own purpose in connecting with you; therefore, just like humans, some may not feel it necessary to connect. They may see that you are doing fine and want you to just continue carrying on with your life. They may be focusing their attention on other people. They may be learning the ropes in their new "home." OR, they may be sending you messages, and you just aren't picking them up because they are different than the way the other Spirits are sending them to you.

Is there a way to prepare our loved ones with how we would communicate to them after death? I think that many people make agreements before a person transitions... something like, "OK, when you get to the Spirit world, show me a butterfly, and I will know it is you." Certainly you can make those kinds of suggestions. However, stay present for all of the ways they might be communicating with you - and not just ONLY that one way that you talked about. Once they go home, they have to learn to focus their attention enough to get us those messages, and sometimes in the beginning there are ways that might be easier for them. I have had many clients that are looking for only one sign and they miss the ten others... so just be sure to stay open for any and all signs.

Do Spirits come around when we think of them? Yes, if we are thinking about them, you can line your energy up to allow yourself to see or feel them. However, when your loved one comes into your mind or heart, seemingly out-of-the blue... then that's them sending you a hello. You believe it is you thinking of them all of a sudden, because your mind took you there; but Spirit tells me that that is when they are sending you a hello... and you receive it.

Some loved ones in Spirit feel close and some feel moved on… why? This is because some really are still closer, and some have moved on. It makes no difference how long they have been gone either. Sometimes people will think that because one Spirit passed away 5 years ago and one passed away 2 years ago, that the one that has passed most recently should stay there longer. That is not the case. It is really dependent on their journey, not on time. Remember, there is no time in the Spirit world.

How can I get concrete proof that anyone can communicate with a loved one after they have passed? I think the best way to get concrete proof is to have your own experience. That can be truly an experience on your own by opening up to receiving a message from your loved one, OR by going to a Medium and allowing the loved ones to come through. The way it will be concrete is that during the reading you will hear things that validate that it is your loved one… but most importantly, you will FEEL the

TRUTH of the message they are giving you throughout your body.

What if the person that has passed didn't speak English, can a Medium still communicate with them? It really doesn't matter because as a Medium connects with that spirit, they connect mostly through thoughts and feelings, which the medium them interprets. Therefore, someone that spoke Russian can still communicate with a Medium that only speaks English.

Why, in my case, do they show up in dreams to talk to me? The dream state is the time when the physical being is in the highest vibration and lacks resistance. Therefore, it is the easiest time/space for the Spirits to connect with them. Communication starts through the dream state for many, but most people don't realize that it is Sprit communication. They think they are just having a dream about them. Dreams are the most effortless way for Spirits to connect because they don't have to lower their vibration for us to "feel" them. When we sleep, our vibration raises. So it is a simpler way to achieve communication, especially when they have first transitioned. It is very common in the first few months for people to have dreams of their departed loved ones. Once those loved ones begin to heal and grow and expand, they learn new ways to communicate, and begin to express in those ways. They start coming through by showing signs like a butterfly, a rose or a heart... they will ring your phone and no one is there or better yet, a call comes from their old number... they'll push pictures off the shelves... they'll send you impressions in your heart ,mind and body. So, they begin to leave messages in the physical world in a variety of new ways. It's like as they learn more in their new world, they evolve from showing up in the dream state to other means of communication.

Do we incarnate immediately? In "earth" time, how long does it usually take? I don't believe there is an average amount of "time" that it takes to incarnate. Each soul has its own journey and so there is not a way to measure the "time" it takes for them to complete it. My sense is that once they are complete with one aspect of expansion, they incarnate to create more opportunities for expansion. When they die, they may be in the "Spirit World" for what we call 10 years or 100 years. When they are complete with that aspect of expansion, they can return again. Or they could also go to other realms to expand. This physical earth is not the only choice.

This part has always confused me: If my loved ones have moved on to another physical life, will they stop communicating with us? I understand how it can be confusing. No, they do not stop communicating with us; because that aspect of their soul still lives on. So, they can be reincarnated into another body, but they still retain all of the knowledge and information of the lives they have lived. Therefore, they can still communicate with you or a Medium.

Are our loved ones with us years after they have passed? I've heard they go to a different dimension. I'd sure like to think my dad is still here to chat with and I feel he is. Yes, our loved ones can be with us years after they pass. They aren't usually with us as often because they do continue to grow and learn in the Spirit world, but they can connect with us at any time. Yes, they are in another dimension, so to speak; but the Spirit lives on, and therefore, he can and will come around and chat.

If a soul chooses to reincarnate quickly, what happens to their ability to communicate and will

a medium know that the soul has already reincarnated? They still have the ability to communicate because their soul is still intact. So, the Medium would tap into the energy of that incarnation. You can speak to a loved one that has passed over and reincarnated because again, all of the aspects of that soul are one. Would a Medium know? They may or may not. It depends on if that information is given to them, was asked of them and/or is important to the client.

If we live many lives (reincarnate), then who are we in heaven? We are not a person, with a name. We are the soul, a vibrational infinite being.

What about suicide? I have a family member who crossed this way. So, when the death is caused by a suicide, how different is the crossing over? Or is it any different? There are many different beliefs around suicide. I'm only going to answer from the perspective of the souls that have passed this way, and not those that are left here. Souls that have passed from suicide typically cross over in the same way that others do. The only difference is that they often spend more time in a "healing space" as I like to call it. In this place, they can help those that are left in the physical, help those individuals to heal, and resolve some of the pain that caused them to leave that way in the first place.

Is their Spirit "trapped?" No, their Spirit is not trapped. They are not any more trapped than any other Spirit. Transitions offer freedom, not entrapment.

How do we communicate with them? You communicate with them exactly the same way you would communicate with any other loved one that has passed on. I think that oftentimes there is so much surprise, anger and guilt about the death that it can feel harder to connect with them initially.

When someone completes their suicide, does the person stay earthbound or do they have the choice between staying earthbound and following the light? I have seen both. Some have stayed earthbound; others have gone to the light right away.

If they have the choice of earth or light, why would they stay and what can we do to help them cross over? They stay earthbound out of regret, out of guilt, out of concern for those they have left behind. Sometimes, I have even had them say that they didn't realize they were dead. What you can do to help them cross over is to send them love, send them light, pray for them, call in the Angels and see them in the truth of who they are - love. Love is what heals: them and us.

Can they guide multiple people or be a Guardian Angel to a new family member? Yes, they can guide multiple people, but they do not become Angels. They can even visit multiple people all at the same time... I have had that happen in my own family. Three different people, in different states, saw signs of my grandfather after he passed at almost the same time. Remember, they don't have a body any longer, so they are not limited to being in one place at a time. They are energy and can be everywhere and anywhere, all at once.

What happens to pets? Pets go to the same place as humans do… and yes, they can be with their loved ones. Many Spirits report that they are with their animals once they return home. All types of animals have come through in readings. I have had horses, dogs, cats, goats, hamsters and even a goldfish. The messages they share are of absolute unconditional love.

Will my deceased pets be waiting for me when I die? This is a resounding YES!

I would ask you to sit down with my dog and figure out whose soul is in there. I swear he has human personality traits. I have experienced where pets take on the energy of different loved ones, but not that they actually are that human soul. A human soul can impress the dog into doing things that might remind you of your loved one, but they do not "become" them.

Could you come back as a dog? Humans are constantly evolving, as are animals. Animals come in with a different intention than those of humans. This is not to say that animals are a lower vibration, quite the opposite. The animals already know that they are love, and they just allow it. Humans on the other hand explore more contrast in order to expand and grow. Therefore, a human would not come back as an animal and an animal would not come back as a human.

What is the concept of time (or lack of time) in Spirit? Earth is but a speck of dust compared to the Spirit world. The Spirit world is an eternal world, transcending time and space.

What do Spirits of your parents do when you are having sex with your spouse? The Spirits watch. They aren't watching the bodies. There is no interest there, as they are not human. They watch the light show. It's a kaleidoscope of color. Sex is a time where our energy is the most focused, the most magnificent and they love the colors of our auras and the heart vibration that occurs.

Do I HAVE to go back to the physical world? You don't HAVE to come back to the physical world, but most souls choose to. We come here to experience expansion and contrast. That is what the physical world can offer in ways that the Spirit world does not.

Can I bypass friends & families and move up to hanging out with Angels, Saints and Jesus and Mary? Is that the top level? Well, I don't know about bypassing your friends and family; but can you evolve to a place of connecting with the angels and saints? Yes!

How do I keep an open conversation going with the Spirit World? Spirit is always communicating with us in all its forms, not just deceased loved ones. You have access to communication with Angels & Archangels, Spirit Guides, Ascended Masters and many other Light Beings. All you have to do is stay connected with them by inviting them into your life. Open yourself up to their guidance and communication through meditation. Stay present in your physical world. Look for the signs from Spirit. They are everywhere. If you keep communicating with them, they will absolutely continue communicating with you. The truth is they will communicate with you even if you don't do anything...but the problem with that is, you probably wouldn't notice.

In Closing

It is likely that this little Q&A book has at a minimum, piqued your curiosity and at a maximum, validated for you that life exists after the physical body dies and that The LOVE Never Ends! My hope is that it has not only answered your initial questions, but that you will also be inspired to ask more questions as you move forward on your journey.

If you have loved what you have read so far, you may be interested in reading my book, *The Love Never Ends*, to which this is a companion book. It is full of great stories, insights, and even quizzes to test your own intuitive connection. Below you will find an excerpt of the book. Please enjoy with my blessings.

~ Sunny Dawn Johnston

Excerpt From
The Love Never Ends

Messages from the other side are our gifts from the spirit world. When we connect, receive, and acknowledge the message, that is our gift back to them. These special messages remind us that our loved ones continue to watch over us. Through interacting with us, they can reveal guidance and information that may only make sense through their eyes, since they can see through the eyes of love.

Remaining open to them gives us the opportunity to do that as well, if we are willing to learn.

Once in spirit, our deceased loved ones see with clarity. There is no judgment or pain because their higher vibration and perspective take the pain away. Things just are. There is no right or wrong. Life can and does continue, but it is our choice about how we continue on . . . in pain, grief, anger, and sadness or in healing, learning, growing, expanding, and loving.

Maintaining a connection with our loved ones after their death can actually inspire us. It can cause us to wake up with joy in our hearts, to embrace life more fully, not push against it with fear. We have an opportunity to live with the awareness that life continues beyond our physical existence. There is not a separation until you create it with fear of the unknown.

My relationships with those who have passed have taught me so much personally: Welcome the life you have yet to live, and appreciate every moment of every day. See and feel how important it is to be present in each and every one of those memories. Love yourself and each other, without condition. Forgive yourself and one another by realizing that there truly is nothing to forgive.

We have all cast the perfect characters for our life experiences. Those who have filled an important role in our lives are playing the part that we ourselves called forth, so as to learn even more about love. Remember that even the uncomfortable experiences in life teach. They may have taught you what you didn't want, which still provides evidence and clarity for what you *do* want . . . and gets you closer to it. That is a tremendous gift.

And our learning doesn't end there. The spirit world is a mental world, so after this life our thoughts will create our afterlife experiences. Once there, you will continue to learn and grow, creating new experiences beyond what you ever imagined in the physical world.

We are reminded by Spirit every day that we are love and are loved. We are loving beings in a physical world that are connected to an afterlife that does indeed exist. (I have never been able to get an address to where the afterlife resides, per se, but it is everywhere. It's in the stars and walking alongside us. It's literally everywhere.) We have all around us this amazing team of deceased loved ones, spirit guides, angels, archangels, ascended masters, and the Divine. They are just waiting for us to ask for help, to allow them in, to truly hear them. They are standing beside you right now. Can you feel them? They are the whisper in your ear, the chills down your spine. They are the presence beside you and the vision in your mind. They are ready to begin this new and expanded journey. Are you?

It is possible to let go of fear and realize that it is only an illusion of great power that prevents us from fully living. Every-one dies, but not everyone really lives. Communicating with the spirit world will allow your soul to open up. You will feel connected, guided, and even exhilarated.

You will begin to understand that everything here on Earth is imperfectly perfect. You will know that your loved ones in spirit see what is invisible to your eyes. You will recognize that everything is in perfect divine order. Everything, including death, is in perfect order.

Spirit is always communicating with us in all its forms, not just through our deceased loved ones. You have access to communication with angels and archangels, spirit guides, ascended masters, and many other light beings. All you have to do is stay connected with them by inviting them into your life. Open yourself up to their guidance and communication through meditation. Stay present in your physical world. Look for the signs from Spirit. They are everywhere. If you keep communicating with your guides, they will absolutely continue communicating with you. The truth is, they will actually try to communicate with you even if you don't do anything . . . but the problem with that is, you probably wouldn't notice.

If you will connect with them long enough, you might even realize that there is no real moral code in the spirit world. By letting go of the judgment of right and wrong, this awareness could create more freedom than you have ever experienced. You don't have to wait to die to feel freedom! You don't have to wait to die to feel absolute, unconditional love. Love is who you are and what you are made of. You don't have to wait until you die to feel and know these things . . . but you can. The choice is up to you. It is OK to wait, but why wait? Why not embrace it all now? Either way, your loved ones will be there, waiting for you and loving you all the way!

So, are you ready to live your life for this moment? Are you ready to pay tribute to your deceased loved ones by living full out? And by full out, I mean loving, every step of the way. Not hiding behind fear any longer, but instead standing up and stepping into the unknown. You are Spirit embodied. You have the knowledge. You have the connection. You have the love. You have your loved ones waiting for you. What more do you need? A little push? You got it.

Ready or not, let's do it. Let's jump in and create the life you truly desire: a life of love and joy and connection. Let's live from a place of love. Let's be willing to ask for and receive help from the spirit world. It starts today! Are you in? Yes!

I'll see you there . . . where the love never ends!

I'm so happy you enjoyed *Answers about the Afterlife*. Please don't forget to check out the inspiration behind this book *The Love Never Ends: Messages from the Other Side*.

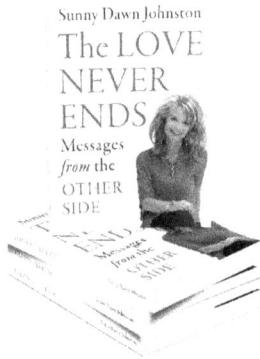

Thank you so much for your support. If you want to continue the conversation, join our interactive Afterlife Facebook community here: https://www.facebook.com/groups/TheAfterlifeStudywithSDJ

About The Author

Sunny Dawn Johnston is an internationally renowned Angel Communicator, author, inspirational speaker and gifted psychic medium. At the age of 13, Sunny began a relationship with Archangel Michael, which helped her to recognize her sensitivity and need for support from something greater than herself. As a teenager she possessed an innate wisdom, awareness and curiosity of the Angelic realm and Spirit world. While she fought those gifts for many years, Spirit ultimately won, and today Sunny is dedicated to teaching others about the Angels, Spirit world and unconditional love. Over the last fifteen years, Sunny has performed thousands of readings and workshops where she's communicated with angels, guides and loved ones who have crossed over to the Other Side. The constant theme she receives from all of these divine entities and loved ones is: The Love Never Ends!

For more information about Sunny's events, classes and services please go to www.sunnydawnjohnston.com.

To check out her amazing SDJ line of books, CDs, jewelry, Teez, oils and lots more, please check out: www.sunnydawnjohnstonboutique.com.

OTHER BOOKS BY
SUNNY DAWN JOHNSTON

Find Me

Invoking the Archangels

Invoking the Archangels Workbook

Living Your Life Purpose with Sunny Dawn Johnston
& Friends

No Mistakes

The Love Never Ends

The Wedding Officiant's Manual

365 Days of Angel Prayers

Healing Mandalas Coloring Book

Archangel Michael: Maintain Your Energy

**For more products by Sunny Dawn Johnston,
please visit:**

www.sunnydawnjohnstonboutique.com

www.ingramcontent.com/pod-product-compliance
Lightning Source LLC
Chambersburg PA
CBHW071431040426
42445CB00012BA/1340